# Wedges in Action

Gillian Gosman

PowerKiDS press.

New York

Published in 2011 by The Rosen Publishing Group, Inc.
29 East 21st Street, New York, NY 10010

First Edition

Editor: Maggie Murphy
Book Design: Kate Laczynski
Photo Researcher: Jessica Gerweck

Photo Credits: Cover, pp. 4, 6, 7, 16–19, 22 Shutterstock.com; back cover and interior cement background graphic © www.iStockphoto.com/walrusmail; back cover and interior graphic (behind some images) © www.iStockphoto.com/Ivan Gusev; p. 5 © www.iStockphoto.com/Simon Podgorsek; p. 9 Ariel Skelley/Getty Images; p. 10 © www.iStockphoto.com/Ina Peters; p. 11 © www.iStockphoto.com/Rob Cruse; p. 12–13 SSPL/Getty Images; p. 14 DEA/A. Dagli Orti/De Agostini/Getty Images; p. 15 Kean Collection/Getty Images; pp. 20–21 © Rosen Publishing.

Library of Congress Cataloging-in-Publication Data
Gosman, Gillian.
  Wedges in action / Gillian Gosman. — 1st ed.
      p. cm. — (Simple machines at work)
  Includes index.
  ISBN 978-1-4488-0683-6 (library binding) — ISBN 978-1-4488-1299-8 (pbk.) — ISBN 978-1-4488-1300-1 (6-pack)
  1. Wedges—Juvenile literature. I. Title.
  TJ1201.W44G68 2011
  621.8—dc22
                                    2009054354

Manufactured in the United States of America

CPSIA Compliance Information: Batch #WS10PK: For Further Information contact Rosen Publishing, New York, New York at 1-800-237-9932

# Contents

# What Is a Wedge?

*The knife this woman is using to cut vegetables is a wedge. The blade of a knife comes to a sharp edge that can easily cut through all kinds of food.*

A wedge may not look like much, but it can do many things! It can cut an object in two pieces, help hold two objects together, or lift a load. A wedge can cut and dig. It can also sharpen, grate, and force objects open. If you know what to look for, you can see wedges all around you!

The wedge is one of six simple machines. It is like another simple machine, the **inclined** plane, but there are a few big differences between them. Though these two machines look alike, we use the wedge and the inclined plane for different jobs and in different ways.

*An ax that you use to chop wood is another kind of wedge.*

# The Parts of a Wedge

*A shovel is a type of wedge that is used for cutting into the ground and lifting up soil. It is wide at the top where it connects to the handle and becomes narrower along the edge used for digging.*

A wedge is a triangular tool, generally made of metal, wood, or plastic. One end is wide. The other end comes to a point or a sharp edge. A wedge is a kind of inclined plane that moves. Inclined planes generally stay in one place.

The pointed tip of a woodpecker's beak cuts into the tree when it pecks at it. Woodpeckers then use their long tongues to feed on insects in the holes they have made.

A wedge may be attached to a handle, as is the case with an ax, a shovel, and a knife. It may be hammered into place, as a nail is, to hold two pieces of wood together. Wedges are also found in nature. Your front teeth are wedges that cut food. A woodpecker's beak is a wedge when it pecks a tree.

Have you ever seen a dog digging in a garden or a backyard? A dog's front paws are very similar to shovels. They are wedges that cut into the ground and lift up soil.

# Making Work Easier

Wedge

Object

Simple machines, such as the wedge, help make work easier. We **apply effort** to the machine, and the machine multiplies, or increases, the power of that effort. Our increased effort is also called force. This force must be greater than the **resistance** of

Here, the top arrow in this diagram shows the downward direction of the force as it is applied to the wedge. The bottom arrows show the side-to-side direction of the force of the wedge as it splits an object.

the object we are trying to cut, move, or hold together.

We call the help that the machine gives us the mechanical advantage of the machine. The longer and thinner a wedge is, the greater its mechanical advantage. A shorter, thicker ax may split a log faster, but it takes greater effort on the part of the person using it.

These girls are using a nail to hold two pieces of wood together. Nails are wedges that are commonly used for this purpose.

9

# A Wedge at Work

The downward force of an ax can quickly split a piece of wood into two pieces!

A wedge works by changing the direction of the force applied to it. For example, an ax is swung down toward a piece of wood. The force of the swing is directed down. The thin edge of the wedge cuts the wood by directing the force sideways into the wood.

A rubber doorstop is another example of a wedge. When you slide a doorstop under a door, the force of your action travels **horizontally**, or in line with the floor. The shape of the wedge and the **friction** created by moving the rubber against the floor changes the direction of the force and keeps the door in place.

*This doorstop is made of wood instead of rubber, but it does the same thing a rubber doorstop does.*

# The First Wedge

Wedges, such as teeth, nails, and claws, have always existed in nature. However, no one can say who the first person to make a wedge was. People around the world have used manmade wedges for millions of years.

Early people living in Africa around 2.6 million years ago used stone hand axes to cut and split food, tree branches, and other natural objects. These hand axes were made by carefully chopping away at one rock with another, stronger rock until the first rock had a narrower edge. These early tools were small,

*This is a hand ax made from a hard stone called flint. It was used in northern Egypt between 9000 and 2700 BC.*

teardrop-shaped objects without handles. However, over time, stone wedges became larger, stronger, and harder to make. They also spread to peoples around the world. **Archaeologists** have found these tools in Europe and Asia.

# Wedges Through Time

*These metal axes were found in present-day Italy. Archaeologists think they may have been used by the Hallstatt peoples during the Iron Age. These axes most likely had handles when they were used.*

There are many examples of early wedges. The ancient Egyptians used a metal wedge called a **chisel** to **quarry** many of the softer stones used to build the great **tombs**, pyramids, and statues of their time. Native Americans also used wedges made from animal bone to cut wood used to build their boats and homes.

Even the earliest farmers used large, curved metal wedges, pulled by horses or other work animals, to plow their fields. A plow cuts long lines in the soil, called furrows, and gets it ready for seeds to be planted. The earliest woodsmen used axes mounted on handles to cut down trees and chop wood.

This picture shows Native Americans holding different kinds of weapons. Their axes, spears, and arrows are all wedges!

# Wedges Today

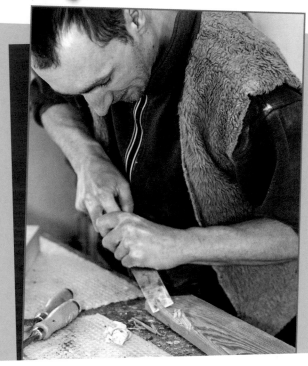

*Here, a woodworker is using a chisel to shape a piece of wood.*

Wedges are used in many modern **industries**, too. Woodworkers and **stonemasons** use chisels. Generally, woodworkers start out using a large chisel to cut away big pieces of wood and then smaller chisels to shape the wood. Woodworkers also use plenty of nails, a type of wedge that holds two things together.

Wedges are also used in farming and building. Earth-moving machines, such as backhoes and plows, use wedged scoops to cut into and move the ground. A simple shovel does the same work.

*One type of chisel woodworkers use is called a gouge. Gouges, such as the ones shown here, have U-shaped or V-shaped heads and are used in sculpture as well as woodworking.*

# Where Can You Find Wedges?

Have you ever had a piece of pizza? The melted mozzarella cheese on a piece of pizza was grated from a large block of cheese by a grater like this one.

If you take a look, you will see that wedges are all around you! A sandbox shovel and a cheese grater are both wedges. A sandbox shovel is used to dig and lift sand. A cheese grater has a perforated surface, or surface with many holes. On top of the holes there are small wedges that can cut a block of cheese into small pieces.

Where else can you find wedges? When you sit down to a meal, there are wedges on both sides of your plate. Your knife, fork, and spoon can each be used as a wedge, scooping or cutting your food into bite-sized servings.

*The small pointed parts of a fork, called tines, are each a single wedge. These wedges cut into your food so that you can pick it up and lift it to your mouth.*

*The sliding part of a zipper has tiny wedges inside it. These wedges draw the teeth of the zipper together or push them apart to close or open your jacket.*

# An Experiment with Wedges

Wedges make cutting or holding objects together easier. You can do a simple **experiment** to see for yourself. Be sure to do this experiment with an adult's help because nails are very sharp and hammers are very heavy.

What You Will Need:
- a bolt
- a nail
- a hammer
- a piece of wood
- an adult to help you

step 2

1. With an adult's help, try to hammer the bolt into the piece of wood. Did it work?

2. Now try to hammer the nail into the same piece of wood. Did it work that time?

3. The edge of the nail is pointed and sharp. The edge of a nail is really a tiny wedge that cuts the wood and makes space for the rest of the nail to be driven in. A bolt has a flat, thick end. It may dent the wood, but it will have a hard time cutting it in two. Wedges make cutting wood easier.

step 3

# Wedges and Air

The wedge is very **aerodynamic**. This means that it can cut through the air and lower the resistance made by the air itself. The nose of an airplane or jet, for example, narrows to a point so that the airplane can go faster and use less fuel than if the nose were

flat. In this way, it is a wedge that multiplies the force of the engine as it cuts into the air.

The wings of an airplane or jet are also wedges, called airfoils. These wings cut into the air and help the plane or jet lift up and fly. Wedges help planes and jets cut through the air like knives!

# Glossary

**aerodynamic** (er-oh-dy-NA-mik) Made to move through the air easily.

**apply** (uh-PLY) To put toward.

**archaeologists** (ahr-kee-AH-luh-jists) People who study the remains of peoples from the past to understand how they lived.

**chisel** (CHIH-zul) A sharp metal tool used to cut and shape wood or stone.

**effort** (EH-fert) The amount of force applied to an object.

**experiment** (ik-SPER-uh-ment) A set of actions or steps taken to learn more about something.

**friction** (FRIK-shin) The rubbing of one thing against another.

**horizontally** (hor-ih-ZON-til-ee) Going from side to side.

**inclined** (in-KLYND) Having a sloped surface.

**industries** (IN-dus-treez) Businesses in which many people work and make money producing products.

**quarry** (KWOR-ee) To dig out or mine.

**resistance** (rih-ZIS-tens) A force that works against another force.

**stonemasons** (STOHN-may-sunz) People who build walls or buildings by laying down stones.

**tombs** (TOOMS) Graves.

# Index

# Web Sites

Due to the changing nature of Internet links, PowerKids Press has developed an online list of Web sites related to the subject of this book. This site is updated regularly. Please use this link to access the list:

www.powerkidslinks.com/sm/wedg/